Anthology of Contemporary Latin American Literature 1960–1984